TABLE OF CONTENTS

1. Table of Contents
2. Publisher Notes
3. The Think Tank Tutor Ad
4. Featured Poem
5. November Expo Gallary
7. Stories
13. Author Zaneta Johns Ad
14. Featured Poem
15. Juneteenth Expo Gallary
17. Stories
24. Avant-garde Books, LLC Ad
25. Featured Poem
26. Returning Citizen's Event Gallery
28. Stories
34. Daily Desire Ad
35. Featured Poem
36. Returning Citizens Feature Gallery
38. Stories
44. Black Connections Ad
45. Featured Poem
46. Community Events Black Connections attended
48. Stories
54. Black Connections Ads
56. Community Events Black Connections attended
58. Business Directory
61. Magazine Ad

PUBLISHER NOTE

Sandra Wilson, CEO of Black Connections,

My story is of a single mother with four children, who witnessed our community being gunned down in the streets by the police. I knew I wanted to do something for our community, so I started protesting on social media through my pro-black Instagram page. A gentleman by the name of Mr. Dale Dowdie reached out to me and said he loved my passion for our community and wanted me to work on his social media pages. I started working for him in February 2018 managing his regular post of black facts. He saw how passionate I was about the black community, so he suggested I start my own business influencing our community to support each other. Because of this, I decided to set up an Instagram page called Black Connections, which would support black companies only. I wanted our community to have a platform just for us. The reason why I wanted us to have our own platform is that I felt that we needed a place just for black people, black business owners, black organizations, and black events so that we could come together and support one another. This platform was designed solely for the black dollar so that we can unite the community and support black-owned businesses to keep our money within our community. By us building more black-owned businesses and investing in each other we can turn our small businesses into major corporations, thus creating more employment opportunities for the people in our community. When we support each other's businesses we are unstoppable; we can cut down on gun violence and poverty and buy lower-income housing, renovate and create affordable housing for our community. We are the change our community needs, starting with the black dollar recycling with black-owned businesses. The time is now for us to support each other and level the playing field.

I started the Black Connections magazine specifically for the Black Connections Family. It is an extension of the Black Connections core values and mission statement. We are changing the narrative. This magazine will promote businesses, non-profits, authors, and organization events that follow and support Black Connections. This is another way to get the word out about amazing things going on in our community. There are so many successful Black Owned Magazines out there. But what sets us apart from others is we focus on black-owned businesses, nonprofits, authors, artists, and organizations that are not celebrities. They're grassroots organizations and black-owned businesses that are trying to pave the way in recycling our dollars.

We have exciting news to share with you, BC family! Our first magazine, Black Connections featuring Returning Citizens, has been accepted into the Library of Congress! It's been a crazy, exciting summer for us indeed. If you haven't read it, you can buy a copy on our website. Thank you everyone for the constant support, we can't do it without you. Here's to our next issue!

THE THINK TANK TUTOR AD

BOOK YOUR SESSION TODAY BY CALLING 832-324-9048 OR ONLINE AT TUTORTHINKTANK.COM

MELANITE LLC

BY: KHALID KARIM
BOOK LINK: LINKTR.EE/KHALIDKARIM75

MELANITE LLC

THE REVOLUTION WILL BE TELEVISED
AND IT'LL BE ON FACEBOOK
AND I.G.
BECAUSE THE REVOLUTIONARY IS ON OUR SIDE
AND WE'LL LEARN SO MUCH MORE
THROUGH HER EYES,
BRIGHT AND BEAUTIFUL EYES
THAT HAVE SEEN THEIR SHARE
OF THIS WORLD'S UGLY SIDE
OF OUR PEOPLE'S UGLY SIDE,
STRONG AND DETERMINED EYES
GLARING
HARD ON OUR ENEMY
GAZING AT US
SYMPATHETIC TO OUR PLIGHT.
OUR REVOLUTIONARY IS A PRIZE
AND SHE DEMANDS TO BE RESPECTED.
ALWAYS DEFENDING US
ALWAYS TAKING CARE OF US
SHE NEEDS TO BE PROTECTED
BY US!
NOT REJECTED,
BUT CROWNED AN ELECTED
QUEEN.
AND SHE KNOWS THIS
THE BIBLE SAYS SHE'S THE RIB.
THE HEART AND THE LUNGS PROTECTION
THE LINK TO OUR EXISTENCE
PAST, PRESENT, AND FUTURE
OUR REVOLUTIONARY
THE KEEPER OF THE BLACK CONNECTION.

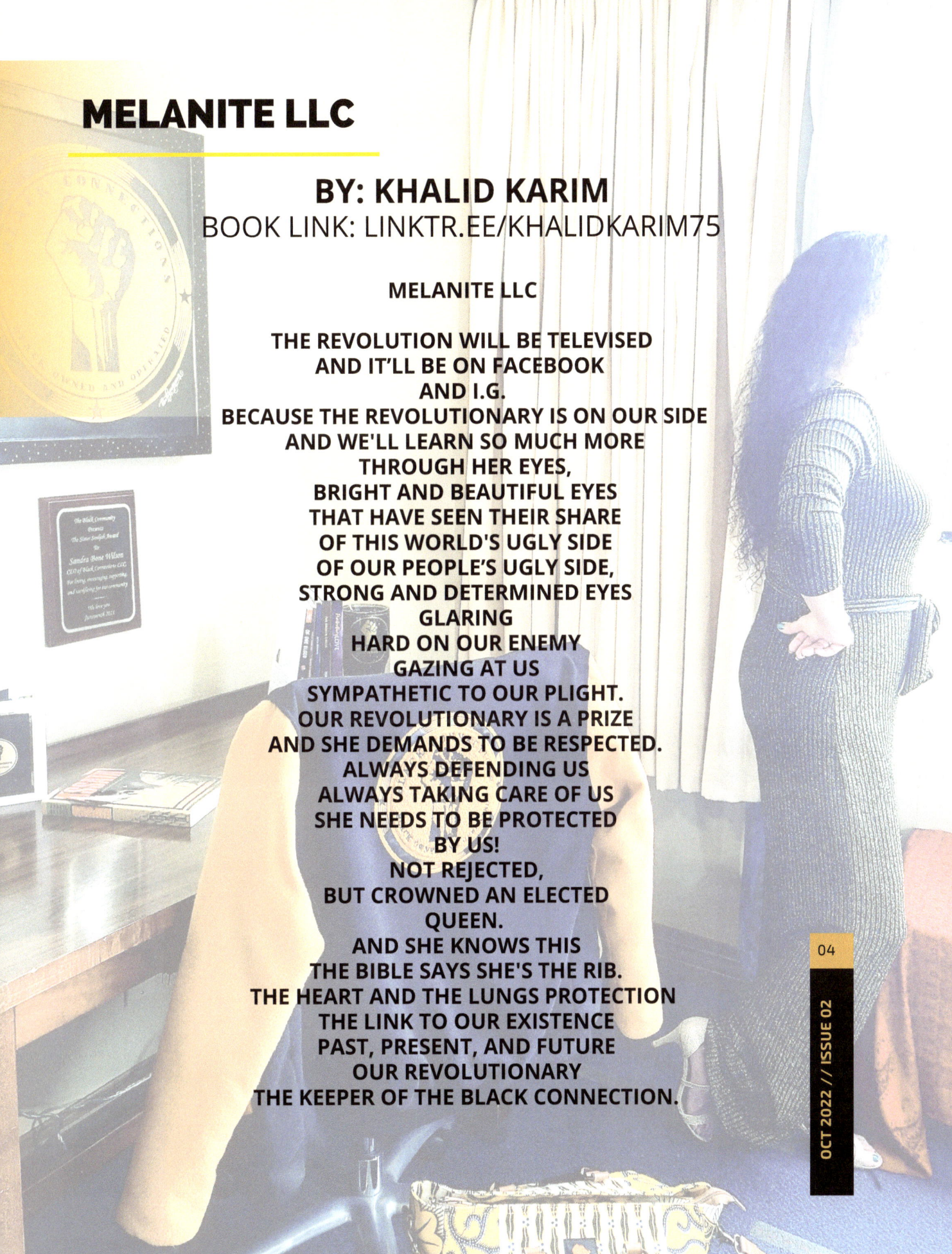

GALLERY: NOVEMBER EXPO 2019

GALLERY: NOVEMBER EXPO 2019

BEHIND THE WRITING

Khalid Karim Washington, DC

Instagram: @khalidkarim75

Facebook: https://www.facebook.com/profile.php?id=100033994352295

Youtube: https://www.youtube.com/channel/UCZEcBjaCv2u-k8W7wwz56Sw

Business Email: b4life1975@gmail.com <b4life1975@gmail.com>;

Who is the CEO of the business?
Khalid Karim born and raised in Washington DC, with a few small stints living in MD., VA.and even St. Croix, has allowed me to live a very diverse life, plenty of good but plenty of bad. And after making bad decisions after bad decisions I found myself in a juvenile detention center a couple of times and ultimately in prison. After serving 25 years of a life and 10 sentence, a sentence that made me evolve from juvenile to man. I eventually became a mentor and since being home I've continued to speak to youth with the intent to make a positive difference for wayward teens. I have started my own nonprofit,"Lessons Learned by Khalid",and with I have gone into a few juvenile detention centers in DC, MD and VA, where I spoke to those youth about the importance of decision making and more.I also have and continue to go and mentor youth in the Potomac Gardens neighborhood in S.E. Washington DC, offering whatever knowledge and wisdom I'm able to.I've also started a YouTube channel where I address real and serious stories about prison, along with the many life lessons I've learned along my journey. I've written and produced 2 books of poetry that I'm proud of and contributed to producing a returning citizens magazine. And I will do so much more...and remain grateful and humble along the way.

What products does your business sell?
I have written and self-published 2 poetry books.

When did you start your business?
My first book was published in 2018, though I've been writing for many years.

Where is your business located?
My first poetry book, "I was just thinking" can be found on Lulu.com, while my second book of poems entitled, "Still Thinking", can be found on Amazon.

BEHIND THE WRITING

Khalid Karim, Washington, DC

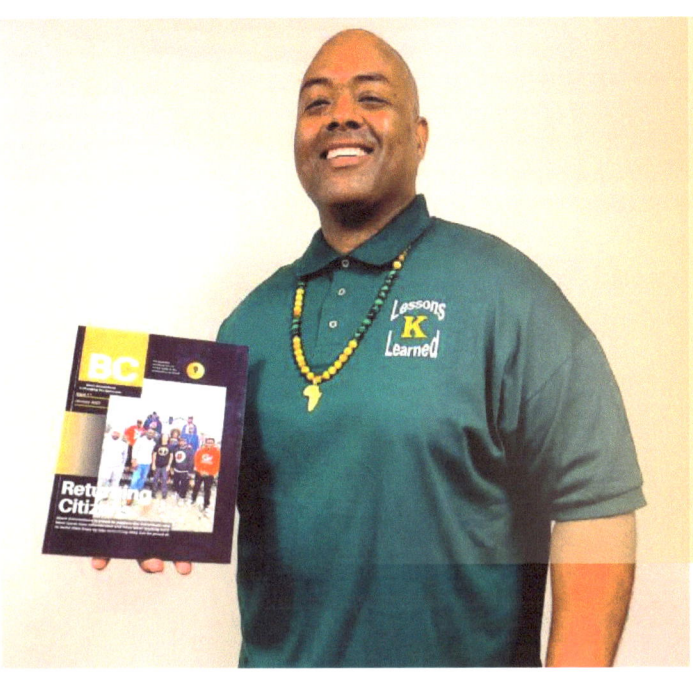

Why did you start your business?
I started writing poetry when I was younger, around 14, trying to rearrange the,"rose's are red, violets are blue..." poem for my mother. I wrote again when I was in the Landmark Detention center when I was 16. Then, after a few people said they liked what I wrote, I continued to write, eventually desiring to write a book.

What have been some of the challenges you have encountered?
There have been many challenges in this process, remaining motivated has been a big one because being incarcerated with a Life sentence, and without knowledge of how to get a book published from inside prison, made it hard to want to continue writing. Another challenge was finding help to type and edit my poems and eventually helping with the whole book formatting and publishing process. And lastly, when self-publishing, promoting yourself is so important but not easy. However, when we listen and learn from the right people and apply good wisdom, things will get done.

What is your favorite part of running your business?
What I truly enjoy most about being an author is when someone tells me just how much my poetry touched them in some way.....or even just having someone purchase one of my books means a lot to me also. But more important to me is simply writing poetry and feeling like it just came out right.

What advice would you give people trying to start your type of business?
For anyone wanting to become an author, I would say, write.. write..and continue to write, your novels, your poetry, your biography, your ideas, whatever but write. And study, because there is so much useful knowledge in books and on the Internet that'll prove beneficial.

If you could talk to your younger self today, what would you tell them?
If I could talk to my younger self about business, I would tell him, "write and keep writing", because all of the other obstacles are out of his control but writing is in his/my control. I would also tell my younger self to learn how to type as well because you don't want to have to wait on others if you can do things yourself.

LAUGHTER: THE BEST MEDICINE

Larry Jones, South Hill, VA

"I get to say yes or no when it comes to my artistry"

Instagram: @larryjonescomedy
Facebook: @hilarryus
Twitter: @hilarryusjones
TikTok: @larryjonescomedy

Why did you start your business?
I started my business because I was already good at making people laugh, I was just able to translate that to the stage and make my living off it.

When did you start your business?
I started doing stand-up comedy in May of 2017.

What type of products do you sell/Services do you offer?
I sell laughter, merch, and a one-of-a-kind emotional roller coaster haha.

Where is your business located?
I work freelance, I can be anywhere at any time…. As long as the deposit's been paid!

What have been some of the challenges you have encountered?
Some challenges have been logistical due to bad weather, other challenges are a combination of creating fresh content while honing my set.

What is your favorite part of running your business?
My favorite part of running my business is that I get to say yes or no when it comes to my artistry. Having a flexible schedule has made life a lot more manageable

What advice would you give people trying to start your type of business?
The advice I would give to people would be for them to chase their dreams until they've captured them.

If you could talk to your younger self today, what would you tell them?
If I could talk to my younger self I'd say, "It's all gonna play out how you want in the end, so keep doing things your way and only your way".

FOR THE CHILDREN

CEO Jessica Montgomery, Waldorf, MD

"**If you don't feel a sense of joy and peace whenever the business crosses your mind...it's not for you.**"

Business Name:
Speak EZ for Kids
Website / URL:
http://www.speakezforkids.com
Instagram:
@speakezforkids

Why did you start your business?
To prepare our children. For college, life, and careers by providing them with foundation tools to becoming effective communicators.

When did you start your business?
7+ years ago

What type of products do you sell/Services do you offer?
Books, journals, and training.

Where is your business located?
Waldorf, MD

What have been some of the challenges you have encountered?
Exposure and support by Parents/Guardians. It's not a luxury program/service. It is a necessity.

What is your favorite part of running your business?
Listening and engaging with the children. Watching them grow, learn, and hold me accountable.

What advice would you give people trying to start your type of business?
Be passionate and committed. It's not something you do just for money. You do it for ministry, passion, and love. If you don't feel a sense of joy and peace whenever the business crosses your mind...it's not for you.

If you could talk to your younger self today, what would you tell them?
Self: Girl! Take a chance! Time and everything else will take care of itself.

ALL IN THE SKIN

Darlene D. Curl, Waldorf, MD

"Constructive criticism helps me improve what I do."

Instagram: @dailydesire425
Facebook: dailydesire425
TikTok: @dailydesire425
LinkedIn: Daily Desire LLC
Email: dailydesire425@gmail.com

Who is the CEO of the business?:
Darlene D. Curl

What type of products do you sell/Services do you offer?
Homemade Skincare Products

When did you start your business?:
April 25, 2016

Where is your business located?:
Waldorf, Maryland

Why did you start your business?:
Originally, the Skincare Creme was a Christmas gift for friends. Upon sharing it with others, there was an interest to purchase. Along with the positive & encouraging feedback received about noticeable skin condition improvements.

What have been some of the challenges you have encountered?
I am someone who doesn't mind experiencing challenges or receiving constructive criticism because it helps me improve whatever it is that I do. I am not afraid to make necessary changes. With that said, when I first started out, I tried to please everyone by meeting their expectations, instead of my own. Learning that I have to spend time conducting the business side of the business and not just spend my time and energy on the creative side of making the products.

ALL IN THE SKIN

Darlene D. Curl, Waldorf, MD

What is your favorite part of running your business?
My favorite part of running the business has to be the interaction I have with my clientele. Whether by email, through social media, or through in-person interactions when I work at vendor events. To see people and get to talk with them about something that has been created from my hands. The joy I receive when they test my product and to see their reactions and hear their on-the-spot review. As well as being able to share my personal faith in God and how it has been instrumental in crossing paths with people, to give me an opportunity to talk about healing one's whole self, mind, body, and soul.

What advice would you give people trying to start your type of business?
The best advice I can give is to be passionate and purposeful with the business you chose to start. The reason is, that it won't seem like a chore when times get rough when you are challenged and want to give up but don't because it means so much and you will do what it will take to succeed. Do your research and put together a business plan before starting. This will assist you in what direction to go in. Don't be afraid to fail and change your perspective when it happens. See it for the opportunity that it is, to be and do something even better.

If you could talk to your younger self today, what would you tell them?
Don't be afraid of what people may think, say or do. Don't allow the negative voices of people who don't understand you and your purpose, (they're not supposed to, because it is yours to bring to fruition), to be louder than yours. Trust and love yourself. You do have the ability to make great decisions, lead others as well as you follow, and most of all believe in yourself and ensure you are taking care of yourself. Strive to stay positive, and learn to be just as good of a receiver, as you are a giver. Stop being so hard on yourself, don't regret the experiences of what you will go through, because the woman you become is pretty awesome!

AUTHOR ZANETA VARNADO JOHNS AD

> We the people were designed to love. It is our faultless virtue and purpose
>
> ZANETA VARNADO JOHNS

Poetic Forecast review excerpt

Ms. Johns' voice is so authentic that you feel like you are her best friend, sitting across from her at the kitchen table as she speaks her heart to you. I have only had her book for a couple of weeks now, but it has already been for me a source of laughter, comfort, and strength.

This book has given me life and hope. It's well written and truly an inspiration.

After the Rainbow review excerpt

"Zaneta has curated her own work and given us the key to a journey steeped in wisdom and love... I could feel the love and wisdom she poured into every line... it literally feels as if she has set aside a comfy chair reserved just for you... Each delivers a message that lingers in your consciousness long after you have closed the book. Later, as you return to that same poem, you are struck by the deeper meanings that emerge.

... It's impossible to have a favorite because the poems are so relatable. (I challenge you to try!)
Emma Selby-Brodie, Host
Just Folks, Conversations with Emma

Your writing is the truth at work. Write on.
David Martin, Founder and Editor
Fine Lines Literary Journal

- in ZanetaVJohns
- f zanjohns.1
- @authorzanjohns
- @ZanJohns1
- g Zaneta Johns

www.zanexpressions.com

HOPELESS ROMANTIC

BY KHALID KARIM
BOOK LINK: LINKTR.EE/KHALIDKARIM75

HOPELESS ROMANTIC
IT WAS THE SMILE THAT GRABBED ME.
ON A FACE THAT ATTRACTED ME
PLEASE TAG ME
WARRIOR QUEEN,
BRIGHT EYES AND A MEAN PHYSIQUE
THAT I LOVE TO HUG.
BUT YOUR PAIN STIRS THE INNER THUG.
ONLY QUIETED BY THE REASSURANCE IN YOUR HUG.
STILL, YOU NEED PROTECTION
AND NOT FROM OUTSIDE TRANSGRESSION
BUT FROM THAT GOLDEN HEART WITHIN.
THAT FOOLS WOULD ABUSE IF THEY COULD
SO, ANY APPROACH IS UNDER INSPECTION.
AND SILLY INTENTIONS
WILL FACE REJECTION.

BUT IS THAT WHY I'M INVESTED?
IS IT YOUR LIPS THAT YEARN TO BE TESTED?
AND I WANNA TASTE.
OR WHEN YOUR HIPS SWAY
AND MY HEARTBEATS ARRESTED?
BUT I DARE NOT SPEAK
FEAR OF MY OWN PASSIONS,
CRAVINGS AND DESIRED MISBEHAVING'S.
I DARE NOT TO SPEAK
BUT MAYBE MY GLANCES GIVE YOU A PEEK.
MAYBE MY HUGS GIVE YOU A PEEK.
MAYBE IT'S THE WAY I SPEAK,
THAT GIVE YOU A PEEK
INTO THOUGHTS THAT I GUARD SO SERIOUSLY.
BUT MY NOSE IS SO WIDE OPEN, AND YOU SMELL SO SWEET
WHAT IS IT?
THAT MAKES ME WANT TO KISS
YOUR LIPS,
YOUR NAVEL,
YOUR NECK,
YOUR HIPS,
YOUR THIGHS,
YOUR LIPS.
OH YES..
THOSE LIPS.
STRIP!
YOUR CLOTHES,
YOUR LAYERS,
YOUR FEARS.
I SWEAR
WE NEED THIS.
THAT MORE PERFECT UNION,
MERGING.
THE CONNECTION INTENSE,
THE FLESH NEEDY AND THE SOUL YEARNING
FOR THAT HAPPY ENDING.
BUT I'M JUST A HOPELESS ROMANTIC.

GALLERY: JUNETEENTH EXPO 2021

GALLERY JUNETEENTH EXPO 2021

LOTUS MOTHER

CEO Vera Green-Mines, Chesterfield, VA

From her website... *"The Lotus Mother is a certified holistic practitioner who specializes in body defining and spirit empowering movement, holistic nutrition, and oracle counseling. Here you will find a space where unconventional thinking is welcomed in order to illuminate unfiltered openness and honest engagement. We are all spiritual beings having a human experience and I look forward to embracing other beings who are seeking to live their lives to the fullest."*

Instagram: @the.lotus.mother
Youtube: The Lotus Mother
Email: thelotusbarrelife@gmail.com

Why did you start your business?
To be a voice for the spiritually awakened in order to break the chains of limitations and conformity surrounding the mental and physical health of the communities of color.

When did you start your business?
2018

What type of products do you sell/Services do you offer?
Holistic Fitness and Spiritual Counseling

Where is your business located?
Chesterfield, VA

What have been some of the challenges you have encountered?
Holistic Healing is often mistaken as a substitution for conventional medicine instead of being seen as the solution to prevent many of the reasons medical care is needed.

LOTUS MOTHER

CEO Vera Green-Mines, Chesterfield, VA

"Be comfortable with being misunderstood."

Pinterest:
The Lotus Mother
Website:
 lotusbarre.com

What is your favorite part of running your business?
Rising every day and living out my passions. For 25 years I worked without fulfillment. Now I have a purpose behind my actions.

What advice would you give people trying to start your type of business?
Be comfortable with being misunderstood. Everyone will not see your vision or support it. Don't give up if you find yourself solitary at times. You were given the vision for a reason and you can make it come to fruition.

If you could talk to your younger self today, what would you tell them?
Don't let others opinions change your self-perception. Your uniqueness is a commodity.

THE BEST DEFENSE

CEO Kaysia Earley, Ft. Lauderdale, FL

"Prior to opening a solo practice, I strongly suggest working as a public defender or prosecutor."

Instagram: @KaysiaEarleyforJudge AND @EarleyLawFirm
Facebook: @KaysiaEarleyforJudge AND @EarleyLawFirm
LinkedIn: Kaysia Earley

Why did you start your business?
To provide quality legal representation in private practice to various clients including indigent and pro bono clients.

When did you start your business?
March 2016

What type of products do you sell/Services do you offer?
Legal Representation for Criminal and Personal Injury Matters.

Where is your business located?
Ft. Lauderdale, FL

What have been some of the challenges you have encountered?
As a solo practitioner, I am responsible for the entire legal preparation and representation from investigating the case to litigating a case before a Jury Trial. I'm limited on the number of clients I retain to ensure I'm providing quality legal representation.

What is your favorite part of running your business?
After trying my case before a jury and hearing the words, "We the Jury find the Defendant 'Not Guilty!"

What advice would you give people trying to start your type of business?
Prior to opening a solo practice, I strongly suggest working as a public defender or prosecutor. The experience gained will be valuable when you begin your private practice.

If you could talk to your younger self today, what would you tell them?
Explore the world as opposed to spending money accumulating unnecessary stuff, items are temporary and memories last a lifetime.

OH, BARTENDER!

CEO Jennifer Bridges Richmond, VA

"The J Bar bartenders are here to assist you with all your mobile bartending needs!"

Business Name: The J Bar Mobile
Instagram: : The_J_Bar_byjenafa
Facebook: : The J Bar Mobile Bartending
Email: Thejbarbyjenafa@gmail.com
Phone: 804-502-3177

When did you start your business?
Started the mobile bartending business in February 2018

What type of products do you sell/Services do you offer?
Here's what we offer: Specialty Bars, Margarita Towers, Corporate Virtual gatherings and demo, Express Mobile Bartending Class, Free Consultation, Actual Bar - fully decorated, Multiple Bartenders, Custom Unique Drink Menu, Bar tools, All Mixers Juices/Soda Garnishing for toppings, AND MORE. Contact us to request a quote and secure your date!

Where is your business located?
We are located in Richmond, VA.

What is your favorite part of running your business?
We are a Brother and Sister Team. Professionalism and good energy are what make us so GREAT. Our bar experience is unmatched. The J Bar bartenders are here to assist you with all your mobile bartending needs! Let The J Bar bartend at your next event. Every J Bar EXPERIENCE is personalized to your taste.

THE CREDIT GURU

CEO Jacci Philpot Fayettville, NC

" You'll see hard times and bad days, but that's what makes it worth it."

Instagram @allaboutcreditllc
Facebook All About Credit LLC

Business Name All About Credit LLC
Business Email afafaync@gmail.com
Phone 407-234-0185

Why did you start your business?
I started the business with my good friend Kiva Israel because we wanted to help our people get back on track. We both have been victims of the monthly payment repair companies, with no change seen.

When did you start your business?
Established 2014, but have worked on credit as a hobby since 2011

What type of products do you sell/Services do you offer?
Credit consultation, credit restoration, and credit course to fix credit yourself

Where is your business located?
North Carolina & Online

What have been some of the challenges you have encountered?
Clients not following specific instructions. If it is not followed completely, you will not see the results you are looking for. Another challenge has been people trying to get over it. I keep the starting score and progression as time goes along. Because I offer a money-back guarantee, some people have tried to get results but a refund at the same time.

What is your favorite part of running your business?
Seeing people achieve their credit goals. I feel like I am purchasing the home, car, and land with them.

What advice would you give people trying to start your type of business?
Stick with it! You'll see hard times and bad days, but that's what makes it worth it. Keep growing, there are always changes.

If you could talk to your younger self today, what would you tell them?
Become better organized, do not address everything you see, let your work.

"I HAVE HEARD THEIR GROANS AND SIGHS, AND SEEN THEIR TEARS, AND I WOULD GIVE EVERY DROP OF BLOOD IN MY VEINS TO FREE THEM."

MULTILINGUAL

CEO Shylene Santiago Cleveland Ohio

"You have to understand your mission is vital to our children's futures."

Instagram: @Learnalanguage4fun2day
Facebook: @Learn A Language 4 Fun
Youtube: Multilingual Stars Homeschool
Linkedin: Shylene Santiago

What products does your business sell?
Bilingual Books

When did you start your business?
2017

Where is your business located?
Cleveland Ohio

Why did you start your business?
I started to help children in the Black Community get excited about learning different languages.

What have been some of the challenges you have encountered?
It has been hard trying to show our people that they can learn multiple languages and that their minds are greater than what they have been taught by this society.
Also getting our people to invest in the books we provide.

What is your favorite part of running your business?
My favorite part is when we go to nursing homes and sing our songs for the residents there! They love seeing the children dressed up in their colorful clothes and they love getting hugs and love! Sometimes they ask if they can go home with us.

MULTILINGUAL

CEO Shylene Santiago Cleveland Ohio

Google Business:
Learn A Language 4 Fun, LLC
Business Name:
Learn A Language 4 Fun, LLC
Business Email:
shylene_santiago@yahoo.com
Phone:
(216) 287-0705

What advice would you give people trying to start your type of business?
I would tell them to stay focused on their mission. Always remember this is for the children. Also, read the books "Awakening the Natural Genius in Black Children" and "Countering the Conspiracy to Destroy Black Boys". These books will help you understand what type of society we are living in and how important our children's minds are. There are going to be a lot of unsupportive people, a lot of non-believing people. The majority for me was our own people. You have to understand your mission is vital to our children's futures. You cannot give any of your attention to those who do not support! So stay strong mentally! Make sure you are meditating daily. And apply for grants! Make videos and collaborate with me. We are in this together! Also, make sure you get to know the librarians in your area. And always keep a smile.

If you could talk to your younger self today, what would you tell them?
I would tell myself to stay strong through it all!

AVANT-GARDE BOOKS, LLC AD

CARNIVOROUS

BY KHALID KARIM
BOOK LINK: LINKTR.EE/KHALIDKARIM75

THE GROWL COMES FROM DEEP WITHIN,
THE YEARN JUST AS DEEP.
THE SCENT STIRS THOUGHTS OF SIN.
THE FOREST DENSE,
WOULD-BE PREDATORS PROWL FOR SUSTENANCE.
TEETH BARED WITH INTENT TO USE,
TONGUE SALIVATES FROM AN INTENSE YEARNIN.
PREY SPOTTED.
MY APPROACH CAREFUL, METHODICAL.
ANTICIPATION PRODUCES A GRIN
AND I POUNCE!
PULLING AND TEARING GARMENTS TOO THIN
TO HINDER THE NEED WITHIN.
FLESH BENEATH MY TEETH YIELD,
QUIVERING WITHIN MY GRIP.
SENSUAL SOUNDS,
SO MANY FEELINGS
AND THOUGHTS WAR WITH THEM.
PASSION AND GREED URGE
WHILE HUNGER DEMANDS NOURISHMENT
QUENCHING MY THIRST UNTIL YOU'RE SPENT
BITING, NIPPING, LICKING
SATISFACTION THE DESTINATION
PREDATOR BECOMES PREY
PREY BECOMES PREDATOR
AND BOTH LAY DEVOURED IN THE END.

GALLERY: FEBRUARY RETURNING CITIZENS EVENT 2022

GALLERY: FEBRUARY RETURNING CITIZENS EVENT 2022

MUSIC IN THE SOUL

CEO Ellis Williams, Richmond, VA

"Don't compromise on your business ethics."

Facebook: @Ewillzmusic

Instagram: @Ewillzmusic

TikTok: @Ewillzmusic

Twitter: @Ewillzmusic

Youtube: youtube.com/user/ewillsmusic

Why did you start your business?
I started my business to engage with my fanbase while inspiring other musicians and creatives to go for their dreams. As a full-time musician, I've always felt that there lacked a platform for entertainers and entrepreneurs at the local level. Sometimes you have to take matters into your own hands and create the very thing you're looking for.

When did you start your business?
May 2017

Who is the CEO?
Ellis Williams is a professional recording artist who has earned a reputation as a musician whose music holds no boundaries. A vocalist and trumpet virtuoso, his music commands attention for the powerful energy it radiates. With over twenty-five years in the music business, he has worked with various genres from Jazz, Funk, R&B, and more. The gifted musician stands tall as an experimental artist with an open heart. An Afro Cuban American born in Brooklyn, New York, he now resides in Richmond, Virginia. Music made its mark from an early age; stepping into a recording studio with his mother fueled his musical vision. After obtaining a place at Norfolk State University, he received a Bachelor in Music Media and later a Master's in Business Entertainment from Full sail University. In 2016, "Call the Battle" was released, an eleven-track album with various collaborators; it peaked on the CMJ Jazz charts. Performing at multiple events, he has played at Busch Gardens, and Carnival Cruise Line and appeared at festivals throughout the eastern United States. An informative music artist, Ellis is the producer & host of "Trumpet Vybes," a podcast that explores the world of the music industry through the perspective of a trumpeter. In addition, he shares his talent on Twitch, presenting the live media show "The All-From-One Experience." The trumpeter is also working with "Good Shot Judy," a high octane swing band from Virginia.

MUSIC IN THE SOUL

CEO Ellis Williams, Richmond, VA

Where is your business located?
E Willz Entertainment is a web-based business with operations out of Richmond, VA.

What have been some of the challenges you have encountered?
One of the hardest things I've struggled with as a CEO is staying focused. Not that I've gotten lazy over the years it's actually quite the opposite. I have the habit of doing too much at one time and trying to manage jobs that are meant for a team as opposed to just one person. Another challenge that I've had to overcome was mustering enough confidence to see it through. Building a business is not easy and I am nowhere near where I'd expected to be but I still have the vision and drive to reach the top of the mountain.

What is your favorite part of running your business?
Hands down my favorite part is having the freedom to do what I want. Life might not be lavish and work might not be consistent at times but nothing beats the ability to say that all of this is MINE. I choose my path and I write my own narrative. The only thing that will top the feeling of freedom is going to be the day I'm able to pass all of this down to my children.

What advice would you give people trying to start your type of business?
Don't compromise on your business ethics. The entertainment industry is forever changing and sometimes I get taken aback by how little people care about dignity and respect. Respect can go a long way and the way you carry yourself will get you further than anything else. I choose to treat partnerships and collaborations with the highest level of respect because I couldn't sleep at night knowing that I screwed someone over. It all comes back.

If you could talk to your younger self today, what would you tell them?
Definity to start this business sooner and not be afraid to fail young. I'm not a man of regrets but if I could change anything it would be the way I viewed the world as a younger man. Too many of us were raised to follow certain paths and expectations and that's just not feasible unless you're born into generational wealth.

BEAUTY IS MODESTY

Halima Muhammad North Carolina

Instagram: @Seredbath @Modestyq

Google Business: www.SeredBath.com

Business Email: YourModestyq@gmail.com

Phone: (336) 999-1135

Why did you start your business:
I started my business for multiple reasons during 2009, when it was not popular in my area to be a black business owner. One reason I started a business was associated with the skin issues my children and I suffered from. At that time, I was on a serious health regimen. After reading several books about skin, I was on a mission to prove to our dermatologist that skin issues were associated primarily with the foods you consume...and I was able to prove it through the improvement in my family's skin, after getting great results, with food and handmade skin care products. I began selling these natural products that help with acne, dry skin and eczema. It seems so strange now, but this was back before people realized that oil was actually something beneficial for your face and hair..lol. I remember that people with acne avoided oil like the plague. The second reason was because I was fired and blackballed after standing up against racial injustice at a company I was working for. I had no choice but to do for self!

When did you start your business:
I created three different businesses over the years. The first business I started was in 2009, which included skincare, lingerie and party clothes (obviously before I joined the nation of islam...lol). Later, as a family, we owned a small gift shop and cafe called the TheTreeHouseStore (we paused from this, but I am hopeful to begin again).
More recently in 2021, I decided to go back to my roots with the skin care, as well as modest fashion as ModestyQ and SeredBath, which was designated as a fundraiser for my grandchildren's homeschool.
Minister Farrakhan, during a lecture, once spoke about the absence of real choices in our communities. This is an issue when it comes to how we dress and what's offered in the stores. I am offering modest, youthful and inexpensive fashion choices to people who prefer to be covered...and in a way that is consistent with a righteous dress code. ...something that any woman on the planet could enjoy and it would make her feel beautiful and feminine. I also wanted to encourage dressing up again, especially since the height of the pandemic, because we started resorting primarily to comfort clothes.

BEAUTY IN MODESTY

Halima Muhammad North Carolina

"It's easier to convince someone to love something you feel great about....so sell what you love"

What type of products do you sell: Hydrating water-based moisturizer and bath soap, body scrub, lip gloss/balm, baby skin care, men's handmade cologne and bath essentials, eco-friendly scrumptious scented candles, modest dress garments, luxurious jewelry, casual jewelry, shoes and handbags.

Where is your business located:
North Carolina...but functions as a 24-hour online business @ www.seredbath.com

What have been some of the challenges you have encountered:
The fear of new age marketing. I am extremely camera shy and it presents a serious issue, because people now want to see and interact with business owners regularly. Sometimes it's a little discouraging. I don't have this issue with selling in person...but I cringe at the camera.

What is your favorite part of running your business:
My favorite part of running my own business is my freedom to create, shift or move at my own pace and have the final say. This is important when you want to impact the world, because you don't have to wait on anyone else's approval. Business is so much more than simply selling, business empowers you to influence...and my goal is to influence the sanctity of femininity and modesty from my unique perspective.

What advice would you give people trying to start your business:
It's easier to convince someone to love something you feel great about....so sell what you love, no matter how successful someone else's business path may appear. I love feminine, dainty, sparkly, luxurious things, so it comes natural for me to express the love I have for it.

If you could talk to your younger self today, what would you tell yourself:
Be consistent and know that a successful business does not happen overnight. The Honorable Elijah Muhammad taught us that anything you want to be successful at, you should work on it everyday. He also taught us that fear stagnates. There is so much we would achieve if we were unafraid. Also, when you have an idea, don't delay it. I have watched many ideas that I had come into fruition by a stranger who did not waste time making it happen. Just do it!

INTO THE MIND

CEO Mianca Woodall

"A lot of old protocols are being erased so look into new avenues to take!"

Instagram: @miamia528

Facebook: Mia S Woodall

Business Email: Wheremadigoes@gmail.com

Phone: (216) 798-9626

Why did you start your business?
My children's books are going to be a series to spark travel in our reader's minds!

When did you start your business?
My children's book "***Where Madi Goes, I Go***" was self-published on Amazon in Sept 2021!

What type of products do you sell?
Children's books

Where is your business located?
Online/ Amazon

What have been some of the challenges you have encountered?
Finding the right contacts/ organizations to reach out to.

What is your favorite part of running your business?
The feedback videos! They are so creative and amazing to watch! Certain aspects I didn't even think of as inspiration to other people so that just motivated me even more for the next book in the series!

What advice would you give people trying to start your type of business?
Do your research online via YouTube or podcasts you will find most of your answers. A lot of old protocols are being erased so look into new avenues to take!

If you could talk to your younger self today, what would you tell them?
Dream Big and go hard for whatever you decide to create! Be resourceful and always enjoy the journey!

PODCAST TIME

Shawn Barksdale, South Boston, VA

Instagram: @press4timeeesllc
Facebook: Shawn Barksdale/ en Minutes of Truth
Twitter: Press 4 Time Tees
Website: Press4timetees.com/TenMinutesofTruth.com
Phone: (434) 446-6633
Email: press4timetees@gmail.com 10minutesoftruthwithshawnbarks@gmail.com

What were you convicted of and how much time did you receive?
I was convicted of Arm Robbery and served 14 years.

How did incarceration affect you?
Incarceration affected me in many ways. It made me aware of my surroundings on a micro and macro scale. It gave me insight into how systems are developed and ran. In a place of negativity, it allowed me to develop an accountability for my actions type of mentality.

What was the turning point for you during your time in?
My turning point in prison was when a friend of mines gave me a responsibility that I was not prepared for nor did I want it. But it lead me down a path of caring more about others than myself.

What, if any, was the biggest influence to your growth and development?
My biggest influence to my growth and development was my belief system. I'm Sunni Muslim

What education or trades did you pick up while being in prison?
I gained my GED, took some college courses, and did a host of trades. Such as commercial cleaning, Auto Cad, and graphics communication. I went on to open my own business learning graphics communication.

What was the most important lesson you learned?
The most important lessons I learned are how to be independent coming home because you may have many doors slammed in your face. Learn every trade you can and leverage that knowledge on the institution to learn how to maneuver on this side of the fence.

In a few words, what have you been doing since you got home and how is that going?
I started my own Printing and graphics business called Press 4 Time Tees and a podcast called Ten Minutes of Truth with Shawn A Barksdale. They both are growing and thriving well.

If you had the opportunity to talk to your younger self right now, what would you tell them?
What I would tell my younger self would be to hold on to your innocence as long as you can and watch who you allow to strip you of it.

DAILY DESIRE AD

DAILYDESIRE425.COM HOMEMADE SKINCARE PRODUCTS LAUNCHED IT'S NEWEST SCENT SANDY'S PURPOSE WITH THE FRAGRANCE HYPNOTIC POISON.

NEW SCENT

https://www.dailydesire425.com/

MY DEAREST UNICORN

BY YOUR FAVORITE BUTTERFLY DANIELLE HALL
WWW.THEBUTTERFLYEFFECTBYDANIELLE.COM

A WOMAN WHO HAS A BEAUTIFUL HEART
WHO ALSO HAS FIRE IN HER SOUL
A WOMAN WHO LOVES HARDER THAN MOST
AND HAS MADE HELPING OTHERS HER GOAL

A WOMAN WHO HAS GIVEN OF SELF
SO MUCH UNTIL SHE RAN DRY
A WOMAN WHO HAS BEEN THROUGH PAIN
THAT WOULD OFTEN MAKE HER CRY

NOT JUST PHYSICAL PAIN,
BUT THE PAIN OF OTHERS DISREGARD
AFTER PUSHING FOR OTHERS TO WIN
AND LOVING THEM SO HARD

THE TRUTH IS, DESPITE HOW IT SEEMS
THE FIRE WITHIN IS STILL BURNING
SHE HASN'T LOST THE FIGHT AND THE LIGHT IS IN SIGHT
THE TABLE WILL SOON BE TURNING

MY DEAREST UNICORN, I LOVE YOU TO LIFE AND
PRAY THAT THIS YEAR WILL BLOW YOU AWAY
WITH GOODNESS

GALLERY: JANUARY ISSUE FEATURING RETURNING CITIZENS 2022

GALLERY: JANUARY ISSUE FEATURING RETURNING CITIZENS 2022

PROTECT & SERVE

CEO SGT JO Atlanta, GA

IG: @tgtacquisition.com

Website: http://www.tgtacquisition.com

email: info@tgtacquisition.com

phone: 770-744-6472

Google Business:
https://goo.gl/maps/6ReGdrkB1ETpio488

Address:
400 Whitby Ter, Hampton, GA 30228

Who is the CEO?
Sgt Jo Lead Firearms Instructor Concealed Carry / Home Defense / Self Defense / TEEX Active Shooter US Marine Team Leader Fallujah, Iraq '04-'05 Ramadi, Iraq '06-'07 HIT/ Rawah Iraq '07-'08 Helmand, Afghan '09-'10 Designated Marksman Combat Tracker Federal Security Team member.

What services does your business offer?
LADIES ONLY TRAINING Ladies, we understand!
Sign up for 1-on-1 classes tailored to you or bring your friends! Who runs the world? Handgun Courses Firearms Safety Intro to Pistols Escalation of Force Multiple Target Engagement Room Clearing. RIFLE COURSES Intro to Rifles Escalation of Force Multiple Target Engagement Room Clearing Transitioning Weapons. Active Shooter Active Threat CORPORATE & SCHOOL SOLUTIONS ACTIVE SHOOTER PLANNING INCIDENT COMMAND LAW ENFORCEMENT TRAINING.

What have been some of the challenges you have encountered?
Finding dedicated and consistent clientele.

What is your favorite part of running your business?
Setting my own schedule and teach as I see fit.

What advice would you give people trying to start your type of business?
Always be a student. You can't grow if you aren't always learning. Experience comes in many shapes.

If you could talk to your younger self today, what would you tell them?
Wait for no one. No one will support your dream like you will; so bet on yourself.

SAFETY FIRST

Sam Futch, Tennesse

IInstagram: @Samjtep

Facebook: @samjtep

Twitter - @tep_samj

TikTok - @samjtep

Business Email
samj@tighteyeprotection.com

Phone - 901-270-3841

Who is the CEO?
Sam Futch Owner/Lead Instructor
Former Law Enforcement Officer with 18+ years of experience. Federal law enforcement 2010-2019: During this time with this DoD agency, I was tasked to play an intricate role in the successful organization of a Tactical Response Team, as SWAT Team Leader and then SWAT Commander. Prior experience came from 9 years of local law enforcement working in one of the most dangerous cities in America. Of those years, 7 were spent on the city's Police SWAT Team completing over 200 tactical missions, I was unit lead on Street Crimes, made over 400 drug and warrant arrests, and spent hundreds of hours working DUI/DWI enforcement. Associates degree in Electronic Engineering with several years of managerial and technical experience. Throughout my law enforcement career I have attended and successfully completed two, 1 federal and 1 local, law enforcement training academies, 4 Dignitary/Executive/High Risk Environment Protection courses, 2 Basic SWAT courses, and several other federal advanced courses, which all included firearms, tactics, Executive Protection, hand to hand assault/counter-assault and advanced driving. Team leader for Protective Detail and motorcade movements while overseas in hostile territory from 2013-2014, Kabul Afghanistan. I have received several instructor certifications to include: National Rifle Association Instructor, Law Enforcement and Civilian

When did you start your business?
August 2016

Why did you start your business?
To teach others to save lives by armed defense, tactics, and prehospital medical techniques

What type of products do you sell?
Professional and safe in person, hands-on training services

Where is your business located?
DMV

What have been some of the challenges you have encountered?
Marketing strategies

What is your favorite part of running your business?
Freedom and a sense of accomplishment

What advice would you give people trying to start your type of business?
Patience and drive to see it through and don't be afraid of asking for help.

If you could talk to your younger self today, what would you tell them?
Listen and commit to success, don't be afraid to step out your comfort zone

HANDBAG LOVERS

Lyanu Adegbite Pennsylvania

"There will be challenging times when you may lack confidence in what you create, however, do not forget your "why" and the vision you had when you first started."

What product does your business sell?
Bags and women's accessories

When did you start your business?
2020

Where is your business located?
Pennsylvania

Why did you start your business?
When asked this question, the main summary is that ToTsFrishion was born from a place of pain when my biological mother and godmother both died of cancer. This pain from the incident was channeled into a purpose that eventually led to my story. I realized everyone has a story and ToTsFrishion's desire is to eventually create an avenue for many to tell their stories. ToTsFrishion started out as an epiphany to make a difference in the feminine world. ToTsFrishion integrates culture into contemporary fashion by offering quality bold print accessories inspired by African culture. With the desire to create cultural awareness and encourage every woman to embrace their potential/individual stories, the brand ToTsFrishion was born. The goal is that our products most especially the bags are worn with pride and inspire a cultural conversation while leaving a positive impact.

What have been some of the challenges you encountered?
As a small business owner, I have experienced so many challenges in the past two years of operating the brand. A major challenge I am presently encountering is the ability to balance being an entrepreneur, working as a full-time nurse, and being a student. The workload could sometimes be overwhelming, however, when there is God, there will always be a way. Another challenge, I have encountered in my entrepreneurship journey is the availability of Funds. The initial capital that funded ToTsFrishion was my personal savings. Although I have no regrets and am grateful for the opportunity I have, the long-term goal of ToTsFrishion will be worth it.

HANDBAG LOVERS

Lyanu Adegbite Pennsylvania

Instagram: @totsfrishion
Facebook: @totsfrishion
Twitter: @totsfrishion
YouTube: @totsfrishion
TikTok: @totsfrishion
Google Business - @totsfrishion
Business email- totsfrishion@gmail.com
Phone - (267) 225-3927

What is your favorite part of running your business?
My favorite part of running ToTsFrishion is designing the bags and seeing a community of people believing in what I create and choose to purchase. This not only gives me joy but fulfillment and a sense of purpose.

What advice would you give people trying to start your type of business:
A major and solid piece of advice I would give is to have faith! Faith and trust in the process are crucial in the present entrepreneurship world. There will be challenging times when you may lack confidence in what you create, however, do not forget your "why" and the vision you had when you first started. In addition, start with whatever resources and knowledge you have. You don't have to make it all perfect before starting, because there will be lessons to be learned along the entrepreneurship journey. Lastly, always endeavor to be different; in the way you present yourself and your brand, be unique. Don't try to emulate anyone, stay focused, and take one task at a time. In my little years of running a brand I've learned you might not get to the desired goal as quickly as you want, but once you stay on track while ignoring all distractions and the world is yours. It might take months or even years but never lose focus.

If you could talk to your younger self today, what would you tell them? Girlllllllllll, be patient with yourself and give room for mistakes. Your purpose, life goal, and definition of success might change as you grow older, and that's okay! Your job is not to satisfy everyone, because you simply can't, just stay true to yourself and most importantly God.

FASHIONISTA

Sunny B, Henrico, VA

"Leave YOUR mark on the world."

Instagram: The Sunori Shop

Facebook: The Sunori Shop/ The Sunori Shop, LLC

TikTok: thesunorishop

Business: The Sunori Shop, LLC

Business Email: sunori4u@gmail.com

Who is the CEO of the business?
Ever since I was a little girl, I always wore accessories of some kind, from simple wear to dramatic. I did it for me, I thought it enhanced my looked and how I was feeling that day. You understand what I'm saying?..LOL. When I would go shopping, I had to go to several stores to find my accessories. Even to this day, I'm surfing different shops online or in-store to complete my looks. So, I said to myself, I'm going to create a store that has just about everything!! Cute, rare, sustainable, and trendy pieces for everyone. Sidenote: If the guys want to get a nice hat, sunglasses, frames, or socks, I have something for them too!.. I'm just saying!

I want to cater to everyone, as much as I can. I want you all to have this for generations to come. I guarantee that I have something for every budget. I work closely with a few manufacturers to ensure that no matter what piece you buy from my store you get sustainable quality. If you feel you are not satisfied, I would love to hear from you. You will be issued a full refund. We are constantly adding to our inventory. So, have fun shopping with me, and don't forget to post and tag what were your must-haves!!

What products does your business sell?
Fashion accessories for men and women

When did you start your business?
I launched on March 1st, 2022

Where is your business located?
Online

FASHIONISTA

Sunny B, Henrico, Va.

"Find ways to make multiple sources of income."

Why did you start your business?
I want to have generational wealth and I know I have something that the people need. You don't have to shop everywhere to complete a look. I got tired of that, so I created my own website.

What have been some of the challenges you have encountered?
Publicity and support.

What is your favorite part of running your business?
Seeing the reactions when people walk by my pop-ups or when I introduce them to the website. Their faces just light up...LOL.. that brings me so much joy...

What advice would you give people trying to start your type of business?
DO IT SCARED AND DON'T BE INTIMATED OR DISCOURAGED.

If you could talk to your younger self today, what would you tell them?
Find ways to make multiple sources of income. Leave your mark on the world. Make everyone remember all the good services you provided to them. SHOW UP, even if you don't feel like it.

BLACK CONNECTIONS LLC AD

SHE IS

BY DAVID SANTINO
DAVIDSANTINO.COM

SHE IS...
BLISS IN EVERY PICTURE.
INTOXICATING LIKE EXPENSIVE LIQUOR.
EVIDENCE THERE'S A HEAVEN IS WHAT YOU WITNESS WHEN YOU SEE HER. A TESTIMONY OF FASHION WRAPPED IN DEEP PASSION.
A VOICE FOR THOSE THAT DON'T KNOW HOW TO SPEAK. A BRIDGE FOR THOSE WHO SEEK THE KNOWLEDGE SHE KEEPS. SHE'S BEAUTY THAT THE MOST HIGH CREATED TO WORSHIPED.
IF HER PICTURE AIN'T PERFECT WELL THEN NEITHER IS YOUR SIGHT. HER SKIN GLOWS A RELAXING HUE WHEN TOUCHED BY THE LIGHT. HER VISUAL A STRONG DOSE OF SATISFACTION FOR THE EYES. INSTANT ADDICTION ONCE YOU WITNESS THE STRENGTH THAT COMES WITH HER VIBE. SHE'S SPECIAL IN EVERY SINCE OF THE WORDS DEFINITION. WHOEVER DISAGREES IS FOOLISH AND OUTRIGHT STUPID.
SHE'S A QUEEN. A GODDESS. SHE IS LOVE.
SHE IS PEACE.

COMMUNITY EVENTS 2018 - 2022

COMMUNITY EVENTS 2018 - 2022

THE CITY KIDS

Rashad Patterson Atlanta GA

"Writing a book is a great way to inspire, motivate, and indoctrinate people about different subjects from your viewpoint."

Instagram:
rashad_patterson_
Website:
 www.rashadpatterson.com
Author:
Rashad Patterson
Email : rashadpatterson54@gmail.com

What products does your business sell? The products my business sells are paperback books, ebooks, and audiobooks. All of my products can be bought on Amazon.

When did you start your business? I started my business my senior year in College at Georgia State University in 2018. The C.E.O of my Company is myself "Brandon Patterson ".

Where is your business located? Since all my products are digital I have an online business.

Why did you start your business? The reason I started my business is to change the narrative in Children's Books. I believe urban children need more relatable books to increase the literacy rate in our communities.

What have been some of the challenges you have encountered? Some of the challenges I have encountered are figuring out how to expand my reach as a self-published author and establishing myself as a respected children's book author. Due to the lack of Black male authors in the industry, it's definitely hard to break through and develop a following.

What is your favorite part of running your business? My favorite part of running my business is the process of developing a book from scratch with your own ideas.

What advice would you give people trying to start your type of business? My advice for people who want to launch their careers as self-published author is to follow their dream. Writing a book is a great way to inspire, motivate, and indoctrinate people about different subjects from your viewpoint.

If you could talk to your younger self today, what would you tell them? Some advice I would tell myself is to always keep an open mind and strive for greatness.

ALL BOOK NO PLAY

Shakina Shaw Bronx, Newyork

"Be sure the business is your passion."

Instagram: Author_S.Shaw
Facebook: Author Shakina Shaw
Youtube: Author S.Shaw
Linkedin: Shakina Shaw
Business: Author Shakina Shaw
Business Email: shakina.shaw@gmail.com

Who is the CEO of the business?

What products does your business sell?
Books

When did you start your business?
September 2020

Where is your business located?
New York

Why did you start your business?
I wanted to be the bridge for others by sharing information to sustain humans and their businesses.

What have been some of the challenges you have encountered?
Low to no support for selling books.

What is your favorite part of running your business?
Getting to connect with others.

What advice would you give people trying to start your type of business?
I highly recommend when you start a business be sure the business is your passion. As you will be tested beyond measure but if it is your passion your joy will remain.

If you could talk to your younger self today, what would you tell them?
Well, darling all those books you love to read, weekend trips to Barnes and Noble, and afterschool trips to library will be beneficial in the future.

CANDLE QUEEN

Tanisha Nicole Cyprian Antelope, California

"For people that are trying to start a business, I would say just do it, don't be afraid. Period!"

Instagram https://www.instagram.com/1essenceq/
Facebook https://www.facebook.com/1EssenceQ
Twitter https://twitter.com/essence_queens
Youtube https://www.youtube.com/channel/UCkFCY1DyRfP_7gOBG15_PEg
Linkedin https://www.linkedin.com/in/essence-of-queens-947386210/
TikTok @EssenceofQueens
Business Email tcyprian@essenceofqueens.com
Phone 7074395100

Who is the CEO of the business? Tanisha Cyprian is a wife of 16 years, a mom, and a businesswoman

What products does your business sell? Soy Wax Essential Oils Candles with Realistic Wax Melts on top of each candle to give my customer two for the price of one. Realistic Wax Melts & Special Occasion Gift Set. Each candle is made just for that occasion for example, our Birthday Gift Set comes with a Happy Birthday fragrance Candle, a birthday T-shirt, a personal bottle, a birthday glass, and much more.

When did you start your business? I start my business in December 2020. I wanted a candle kit for Christmas and the rest is history.

Where is your business located? Antelope, California

Why did you start your business? I start a business for two reasons 1. I love candles and I used to buy them every chance I got. 2. My mom use to cough as I was doing my research I found out that candles all have different waxes, and wicks that are harmful to us and the environment. So I use soy wax & essential oil and she stopped coughing.

What have been some of the challenges you have encountered? The challenges that I have faced have been marketing, just because people I thought would help haven't. Don't stop! The ones that matter will be there when you need them.

What is your favorite part of running your business? Networking is my favorite part. I have met some amazing people.

What advice would you give people trying to start your type of business? For people that are trying to start a business, I would say just do it, don't be afraid. Period!

If you could talk to your younger self today, what would you tell them? If I could talk to my younger self, I would say, "stop playing church and pay attention, when someone shows you whom they believe. Love people with boundaries. Train people how to treat you. Self-care and self-love are very important!"

HEALTHY HEALING

Kayshaun Brooks Modesto, California

IInstagram.com/renewyoubodybutters

Facebook.com/renewyoubodybutter

Twitter.com/renewyoubody

http://linkedin.com/in/kayshaun-brooks-bsm-bb858416b

Pinterest.com/renewyoubodybutters

Tictok.com/renewyoubodybutters

Google Business: Renew You, Body Butters

Email: info@renewyoubodybutter.com

Phone: 209-416-7078

Who is the CEO of the business?
Kayshaun comes from a medical background with over 20 years of experience in nursing, mental health, project development, and management. Over the last 2 decades, Kayshaun has studied and used many holistic alternatives in all aspects of her life; medicine, skincare, home practices, and beyond. Her passion for organic skincare started in 2007 when her youngest son was diagnosed with eczema at just a few months old. During her journey, she was able to learn, study and implement alternative holistic methods and avoid harsh chemicals to heal herself as well as her friends and family. Kayshaun decided it was her mission to share this healing knowledge and set out in launching her businesses. She launched Renew You, Body Butters, in 2018 to offer people luxury organic skincare that is ethically sourced and handcrafted. In 2020 her affiliate program took off with much success. She is set to launch her following businesses surrounding holistic lifestyle coaching and mentoring others to start or grow their own beauty business.

What products does your business sell?
I sell organic skincare products.

When did you start your business?
I started my business in 2018.

Where is your business located?
My business is located in California.

HEALTHY HEALING

Kayshaun Brooks Modesto, California

"Why grow your business by yourself when others are willing to help you and you never have to worry about who's not supporting you?"

Instagram.com/renewyoubodybutters
Facebook.com/renewyoubodybutter
Twitter.com/renewyoubody
http://linkedin.com/in/kayshaun-brooks-bsm-bb858416b
Pinterest.com/renewyoubodybutters
Tiktok.com/renewyoubodybutters
Google Business: Renew You, Body Butters
Email: info@renewyoubodybutter.com
Phone: 209-416-7078

Why did you start your business?
I started my business to be the solution I was looking for when I was in need. My son was diagnosed with severe eczema as an infant and suffered for many years trying traditional western medicine techniques. After some years I got fed up and created my own skincare products for him and our family. We have really sensitive skin issues and I couldn't find products for us. After 10 years of creating products for us and those closest to me, I said it was time to help those on a massive scale and start my company.

What have been some of the challenges you have encountered?
The biggest challenge has been building this company managing chronic pain and chronic illnesses without the capability of working a job. I am strictly walking in faith into my purpose.

What is your favorite part of running your business?
My favorite parts of running my business are making skincare products for those who are in need and building relationships with my affiliates. I've truly learned to enjoy networking, collaborating, and building business relationships.

What advice would you give people trying to start your type of business?
I would tell anyone starting a business to make sure they're always networking, collaborating, and building business relationships. Also, start an affiliate program as well. Why grow your business by yourself when others are willing to help you and you never have to worry about who's not supporting you?

If you could talk to your younger self today, what would you tell them?
I would tell my younger self to never worry about who's supporting me and focus on meeting the people who will and want to support you.

MEDIA MANAGER

Chantelle Douglas Princeton, LA

"Stop second guessing yourself, create boundaries and do what your heart deeply desires"

Instagram:
@thequeenofdigitalmarketing
Facebook:
@thequeenofdigitalmarketing
Pinterest:
@thequeenofdigitalmarketing
Google Business:
Write For You Media
Business Email:
writeforyoumedia@gmail.com

What products does your business sell?
I offer social media management, lead generation, and 1:1 consulting services for other business owners. I also provide quarterly promotions, create custom packages for nonprofits, and have a content planning training video for business owners.

When did you start your business?
Unofficially in 2016. Officially registered on February 3, 2018.

Where is your business located?
Virtually, but I reside in North Louisiana.

Why did you start your business?
I started my business because I saw a growing need for more quality representation of black businesses on social platforms.

What have been some of the challenges you have encountered?
Finding my flow and connecting with my soul tribe has been the greatest challenge for me.

What is your favorite part of running your business?
What brings me joy the most as a business owner is having complete autonomy over my life and time. I also enjoy staying home with my sons.

What advice would you give people trying to start your type of business?
For those desiring to venture into the digital marketing industry, I encourage you to get a mentor. Relying solely on a few Youtube videos and Google information will not do you justice.

If you could talk to your younger self today, what would you tell them?
"Chantelle, you are fine just the way you are. You are ahead of your time and there's nothing wrong with that. Stop second guessing yourself, create boundaries and do what your heart deeply desires."

BLACK CONNECTIONS LLC AD

BLACK CONNECTIONS LLC AD

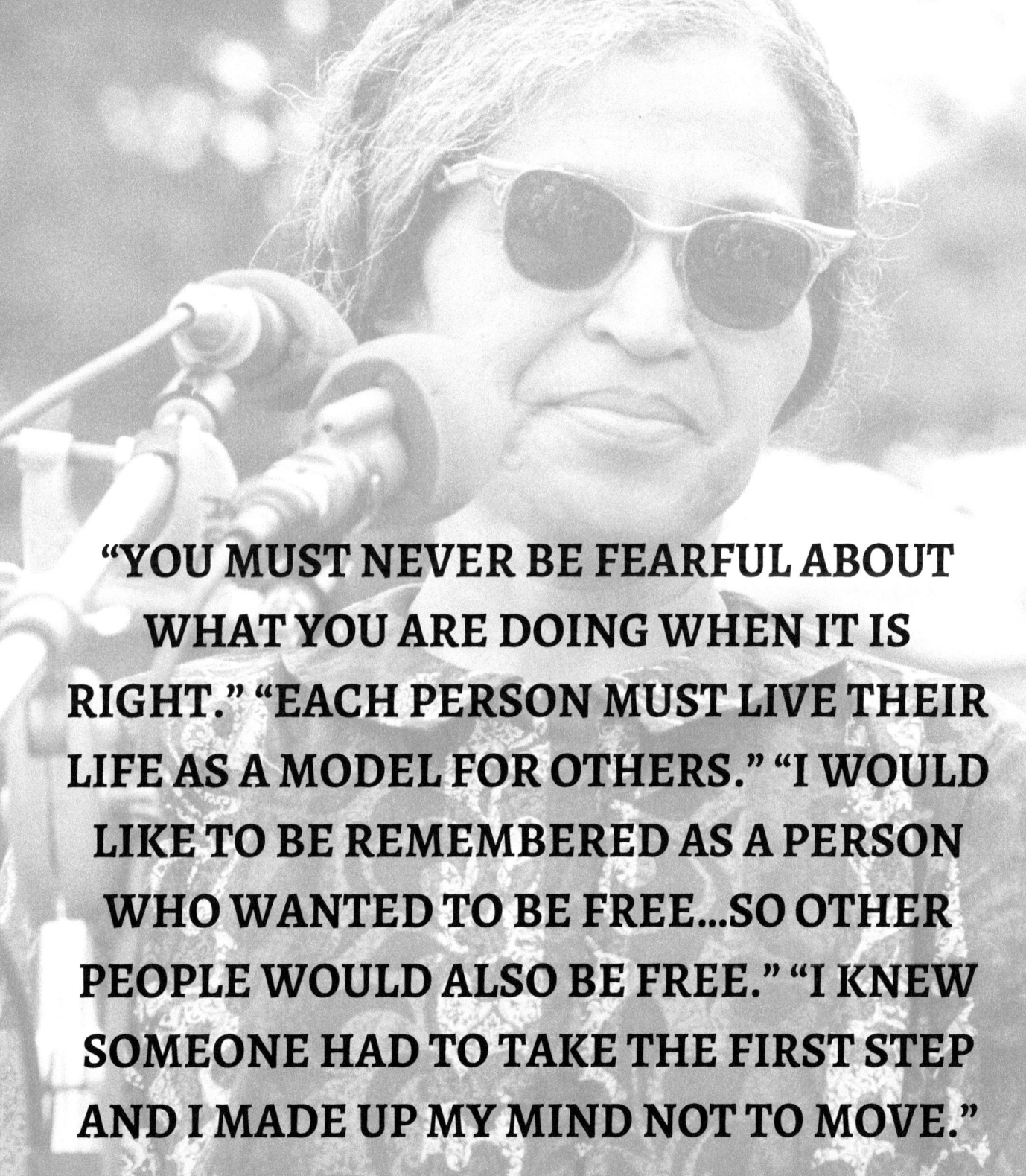

COMMUNITY EVENTS 2018 - 2022

COMMUNITY EVENTS 2018 - 2022

BUSINESSES THAT SUPPORTED BC WHILE I'VE BEEN UNDER THE WEATHER

365 I Women's Empowerment
We create bath and body products that will change your atmosphere. Encounter unforgettable #experiences and feel #relaxed, rejuvenated, and #refreshed
linktr.ee/refreshed365

3kingvisions
Education Librarian Storyteller Leaders of the New Cool Vegas I help kids develop the love of READING!!
linktr.ee/3kingvisions

Affordable Power Washing Pros
Pressure Washing Business Marketing and Training. Affordable Pressure/Soft-Wash Exterior Cleaning Services. Google My Business Organically
affordpressurewashing.go.studio

Author Shakina Shaw
Where Genres Meet
www.authorshaw.com

B'More Made with Pride
A shared kitchen for food businesses and cafes to Eat, Drink & B'More Happy. PopUp: opportunities available
linktr.ee/brittlequeen

Body & Soul Naturally
NonToxic Personal Care Aluminum Free Deodorant~Whipped Body Butter~Sulfate Free Body Wash~Beard Products & More! Illinois Based Co. Fast Shipping
bodyandsoulnaturally.com

Computerology
The Computer Surgeon RVA We Fix Broken/Damaged Repairs +More Monday - Friday:10 am-6 pm Saturday-10 am-2 pm
computericu.com

Dashvisionllc
Dash Vision Photography Videography
www.dashvisionllc.com

Dee F.B. LCSW | Author | Coach
Best Selling Author Trauma & Grief Expert Former Dancehall Queen
Promoting mental wellness by spreading Black Joy with Black Books
linktr.ee/deefbland

Dreamy Treasures Official
Crafter, custom designs, wood specialist. Custom made items from wood, Acrylic, glass, and much more
linktr.ee/dreamytreasures 804-464-8622

ESSENCE OF QUEENS
Soy Wax Candles One Stop Shop I Gift Boxes Bride-to-be Mom To Be Congrats 2 in 1 Candle With Life Like Wax Melts
www.essenceofqueens.com

Gentlemen's Touch Beard Products
LUXURY GROOMING | BEARD PRODUCTS
Bamboo Charcoal based All Natural Ingredients Fast Shipping Treat Yourself
linkpop.com/gentlemenxtouch

Jai'Colby'E | Social Worker
Knowledge is Freedom. Father HBCU Grad Social Worker Self-Published author
LINK FOR BOOK BELOW WITH A FREE eBook
linktr.ee/Jaicolbye

Jeanpierre Spices
Your one-stop Restaurant and Spice Shop.
www.jeanpierrespices.com

BUSINESSES CONT.

Kalunda Janae Hilton
Art, Fashion & Photography
kalunda-hilton.pixels.com

Ko'Kila
Light Switch, Outlet Covers, Wallplates & More
linkpop.com/kustomkreationzbykila

Isimonespiritualcollection
Digital creator Creations to Inspire & Awaken Your Soul.
www.Isimonespiritualcollection.com

Miki Dee Candle Co llc
Scented Candles/ Room Sprays Hand Poured in the Bronx, NY
www.mikideecandleco.com

Mood Room Candle Co
Handcrafted, all-natural, modern, and made with love. Each fragrance tells a story. Find yours. Proud Detroit business.
linktr.ee/Moodroomcandleco

Naija Grill and Spice Mix
Goes on everything Heat & Flavor in a Bottle Say No To Bland Food Glendale, AZ
linktr.ee/naijagrille

Nicole Patrice Thomas
Christian Author of YA Fantasy English/Spanish Diverse Picture-books, Poetry & Journals
www.nicolepatricethomas.com

Novels by Jodaea
P. O. Box 3376 Petersburg VA 23805
www.novelsbyjodaea.com

Olaolu Ogunyemi
U.S. Marine Officer | Mentor | BEST SELLING Author
linktr.ee/OlaoluOgunyemi

Pamper and Beyond Candle Maker
Bath Products Delicious Candles Hand Poured with Love, Peace, and Soul Enjoy 15% off with code: PAMPER15
www.pamperandbeyond.com

PhillyExperiences
Black LGBTQ Hood Experiences in Philly Black Mural Tours Wellness Sessions Themed Party Buses Amplifying Black Philly Together
linktr.ee/phillyexperiences

Ponds Edge Designs
Handmade gifts and beadwork for men women and the home.
www.pondsedgedesigns.net

QuYahni Lewis
Self-healing Coach/50+ Curvy Fashionista/Author/Cohost of the Q&A Exchange, Saturdays @ 6 pm on Reygn TV (via Roku & Firestick)
sites.google.com/view/inherworkelevationco

Read With Carylee
Kid's show #diversekidslit Children's Author/Advocate/Speaker Read with Carylee, YouTube & Podcast
linktr.ee/readwithcarylee

Renewyoubodybutters
Beauty, cosmetic & personal care 20 years of medical exp. Celebrity Trusted Skincare Affiliate Program Private Label Foods That Can Cause an Eczema Flare Up Free Ebook
linktr.ee/renewyoubodybutters

Rodney Cloud Hill
PanAfrikan /G\ Author of "BlackWash: The Untold Stories of Reverse Racism" and "The Cloud Effect" Poet Advocate {D}MV
rodneycloudhill.com

Royal Sutton Body & Skincare
Healthy Hair & Glowing Skin is in! Vegan, paraben-free, cruelty-free! FOR ALL HAIR TYPES.
www.royal-sutton.com

BUSINESSES CONT.

Rubi D.
Loc'd 9.9.2021 @thegoddessgrind @artisticsnaturalbodycare
www.rubidartistry.com/linktree

VINTAGE CLOTHING APPAREL
A Hip Hop & Black inspired clothing line that is true to the culture of VINTAGE. Neva Outta Style.
vintageclothingapparel.com

Yes Bundle LLC
#YESBUNDLE #SCHOOLSUPPLIES K~H.S. Pre-package School Supplies Customized Packages SUPPORT
https://yesbundle.com/

the quarterly showcase for all things black in the entrepenaurial world

BE A PART OF OUR NEXT ISSUE

BE IN OUR NEXT BLACK CONNECTIONS MAGAZINE:
HTTPS://BLACKCONNECTIONSLLC.COM/BLACK-CONNECTIONS-MAGAZINE/

MAGAZINE OPTIONS:
BUSINESS RESOUCE PAGE $10.00
FULL PAGE ADVERTISEMENT $12.00
ONE PAGE INTERVIEW $75.00
TWO PAGE INTERVIEW $100.00

PURCHASE OUR FIRST MAGAZINE FEATURING RETURNING CITIZENS
HTTPS://BLACKCONNECTIONSLLC.COM/BLACK-CONNECTIONS-MAGAZINE/

www.ingramcontent.com/pod-product-compliance
Lightning Source LLC
Chambersburg PA
CBHW041932240526
45473CB00034B/930